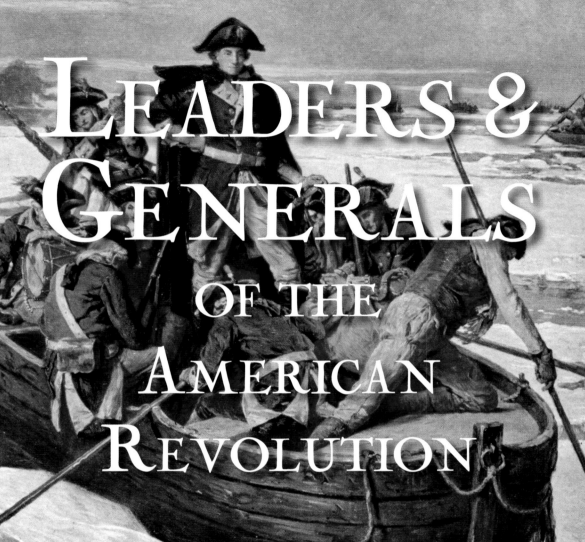

LEADERS & GENERALS
OF THE
AMERICAN
REVOLUTION

By JOHN HAMILTON

VISIT US AT
WWW.ABDOPUBLISHING.COM

Published by ABDO Publishing Company, PO Box 398166, Minneapolis, MN 55439.
Copyright ©2013 by Abdo Consulting Group, Inc. International copyrights reserved in all countries. No part of this book may be reproduced in any form without written permission from the publisher. ABDO & Daughters™ is a trademark and logo of ABDO Publishing Company.

Printed in the United States of America, North Mankato, Minnesota.
122012
012013

Editor: Sue Hamilton
Graphic Design: Sue Hamilton
Cover Design: Neil Klinepier
Cover: Painting by Don Troiani, www.historicalartprints.com
Interior Photos and Illustrations: Brown University Library-Providence, RI-pg 26 (right); Corbis-pg 25 (bottom); Getty Images-pgs 4-5 & 7; Granger Collection-pgs 8-11, 13, 15-17, 19, 20, 22 (top), 23, 24 (top) & 27 (bottom); Military and Historical Image Bank-pgs 6 & 21; Library of Congress-pgs 1, 6, 22 (bottom), 28 & 29; National Institute of American History & Democracry/Artist John Smart-pg 27 (top); Smithsonian Institute/National Portrait Gallery-pgs 12 (Artist John Trumbull), 14 (Artist Mather Brown), 18 (Artist James Peale), 24 (bottom) (Artist John Trumbull) & 25 (top) (Artist Charles Peale Polk); Yale Center for British Art/Artist John Copley-pg 26 (left).

ABDO Booklinks

To learn more about the American Revolution, visit ABDO Publishing Company online. Web sites about the American Revolution are featured on our Book Links pages. These links are routinely monitored and updated to provide the most current information available. Web site: www.abdopublishing.com

Cataloging-in-Publication Data

Hamilton, John, 1959-
 Leaders and generals of the American Revolution / John Hamilton.
  p. cm. -- (American Revolution)
Includes index.
ISBN 978-1-61783-681-7
1. Generals--United States--Biography--Juvenile literature. 2. Heroes--United States--Biography--Juvenile literature. 3. United States--History--Revolution, 1775-1783--Biography--Juvenile literature. I. Title.
973.7/092/2--dc22
[B]

2012945972

CONTENTS

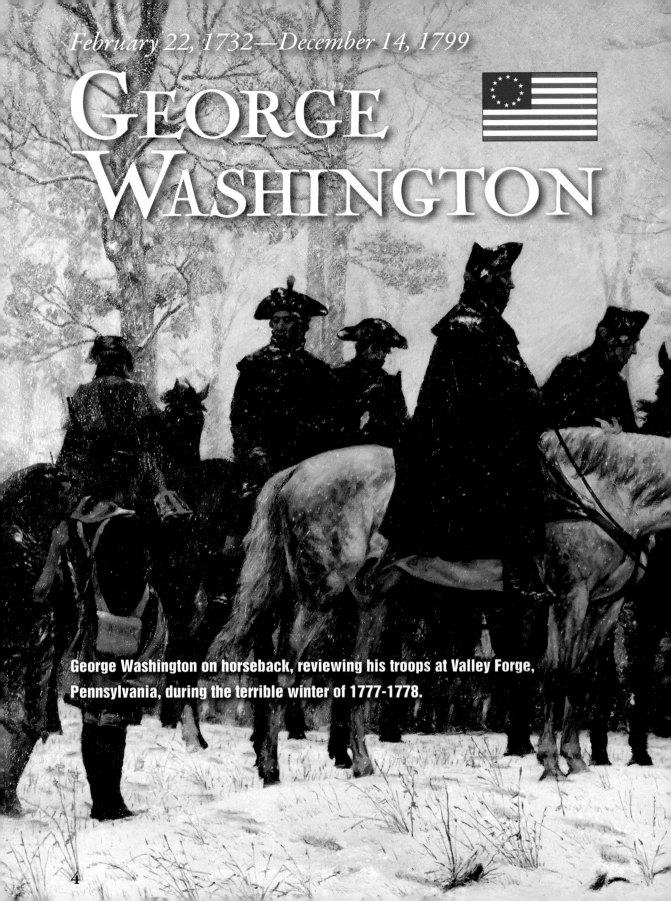

February 22, 1732—December 14, 1799

GEORGE WASHINGTON

George Washington on horseback, reviewing his troops at Valley Forge, Pennsylvania, during the terrible winter of 1777-1778.

George Washington is known in the United States today as one of the country's Founding Fathers. He was commander in chief of the victorious Continental Army, and a two-term president who guided and nurtured his country through its crucial early years. But when the American Revolution began in 1775, George Washington's skill at leading a large army in open-field combat was mostly unproven. Carrying the hopes of a new nation on his shoulders, Washington led a collection of inexperienced and outgunned colonial soldiers against Great Britain, the most powerful nation on Earth. Washington was a courageous and resourceful commander, but as the war began, the fate of America was far from certain.

General George Washington rides beside Patriot troops from Virginia and Pennsylvania in 1777.

George Washington was born in Virginia on February 22, 1732. The son of a wealthy planter, he grew up to be a well-mannered gentleman. He became a land surveyor at age 16. Washington was tall and powerfully built, and he was an excellent horseman. He inherited his Mount Vernon plantation in Virginia at age 22 from his brother Lawrence.

During the French and Indian War, from 1754 to 1755, Washington fought as a lieutenant colonel in the British Army. He learned military tactics as he led soldiers into battle in the Ohio Valley and western Pennsylvania. Washington was very brave. He was also lucky: he survived one battle with four bullet holes in his uniform and two horses shot out from under him.

After the French and Indian War, Washington became active in Virginia politics, but he loved working on his farmlands best. Like other colonists, he grew to resent British taxes and trade regulations, and felt exploited by the colonial system. In 1774 he was a Virginia delegate to the First Continental Congress in Philadelphia, Pennsylvania.

In May 1775, Washington attended the Second Continental Congress. Because of his political connections and military background, Washington was elected to lead the newly formed Continental Army.

General Washington took command of his troops on July 3, 1775, during the siege of Boston, Massachusetts. Washington was victorious at Boston, but the fighting dragged on for six long years.

Through victories and defeats, Washington never gave up. He knew the importance of properly training his troops. His strategy against the mighty British Army was to strike fast and unexpectedly. He was unafraid to retreat when necessary, falling back slowly and inflicting high casualties against the enemy. With the aid of French allies, he won a major victory at the Battle of Yorktown, Virginia, in 1781, effectively ending the war.

Though he had fought for many years, Washington had not yet finished serving his country. His efforts helped create the Constitution of the United States. He was elected as the county's first president in 1789, and served two terms. He resisted political bickering and urged his fellow countrymen to stay neutral in foreign wars.

Finally, in 1797, Washington returned to his beloved Mount Vernon in Virginia. He died less than three years later from a throat infection on December 14, 1799. All across the United States, Americans mourned the father of their country.

An actor stands in front of Mount Vernon, George Washington's beloved Virginia home.

BRITISH LEADERS

King George III

June 4, 1738—January 29, 1820

George III was the king of Great Britain for almost 60 years, from 1760 to 1820. He was beloved by many of his subjects in Great Britain, but hated as a tyrant in America. Before his reign, taxes and regulations on trade goods with the colonies were seldom enforced. George III changed that. His strict policies meant that Americans were taxed, even though they didn't have a voice in the British government. George III continually ignored the colonists's objections. He insisted that they obey his rule. His harsh policies led to the American Revolution. In his later years, George III suffered from mental illness that may have been caused by a disease called porphyria. His son, George IV, took over most of his duties in 1811.

Lord Frederick North

April 13, 1732—August 5, 1792

Lord Frederick North was the prime minister of Great Britain from 1770 to 1782. Like King George III, Lord North tried to make the American colonies obey British power. He also believed that taxation of the colonies was critical to the British economy. Lord North allied himself with the king and others in Parliament to pass laws punishing the Americans. These included the Intolerable Acts of 1774 that followed the Boston Tea Party. Lord North's hard-hearted policies caused much anger leading to the American Revolution. Today he is often known as the British prime minister "who lost America."

PATRIOT LEADERS

Samuel Adams

September 27, 1722—
October 2, 1803

Samuel Adams was born in Boston, Massachusetts, in 1722. He was a brewer, businessman, and writer. He was also a radical Patriot with a brilliant talent for organizing political protests. He was highly educated, graduating from Harvard College in 1740. Adams opposed British tax policies against the colonies. He organized secret agitator groups such as the Sons of Liberty and the Committees of Correspondence. Adams also organized the revolt that led to the Boston Tea Party in 1773.

Adams strongly urged his fellow colonists to break away from Great Britain. He was a member of the First and Second Continental Congresses, and was a signer of the Declaration of Independence. After the revolution, Adams served as governor of Massachusetts from 1794 to 1797.

Paul Revere was a successful silversmith from Boston, Massachusetts, who became active in anti-British politics. He spied on British soldiers, and took part in the Boston Tea Party.

Revere is most famous for his role in warning Patriot leaders Samuel Adams and John Hancock of a planned British military attack on the night of April 18, 1775.

Revere and several others rode their horses through the Massachusetts countryside, warning of a British plan to seize weapons and arrest Patriot leaders. Revere's alarm gave colonial militia time to organize and resist the Redcoats. The resulting Battles of Lexington and Concord signaled the start of the American Revolution.

John Adams

October 30, 1735—July 4, 1826

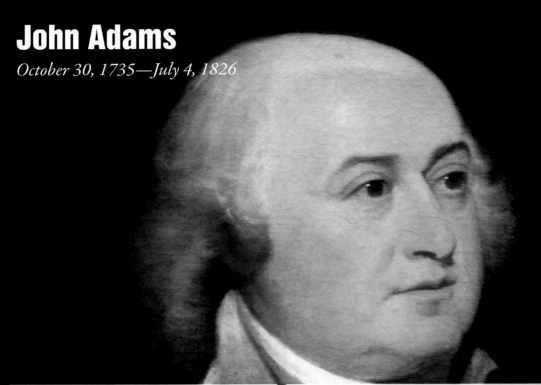

Along with George Washington, John Adams was one of the most influential Founding Fathers. He helped create the foundation of the United States as we know it today. Adams was a Harvard-educated lawyer, statesman, and author. He believed in fairness under the law, and even defended in court the British soldiers involved in the Boston Massacre.

Adams served as a Massachusetts delegate to the First and Second Continental Congresses, helping create and then signing the Declaration of Independence in 1776. In 1782, he helped negotiate the Treaty of Paris, which officially ended the war with Great Britain the following year.

Adams served as the second president of the United States from 1797 to 1801. After retiring from public service, Adams lived quietly on his family farm in Quincy, Massachusetts. He continued to correspond with his friend and political rival Thomas Jefferson. Both former presidents died on the 50th anniversary of American independence, on July 4, 1826.

John Hancock

January 23, 1737—October 8, 1793

John Hancock was a wealthy Boston revolutionary. He earned his riches by running a shipping business. He led a lavish lifestyle, but he also spent his money on projects that benefitted the public. His generosity made him very popular in Massachusetts. His Patriot activities, however, made him a wanted man, but he always evaded capture by British authorities.

Hancock was very involved in Massachusetts politics, which led to his election as president of the Second Continental Congress in Philadelphia, Pennsylvania, in May 1775. As president, Hancock became the first signer of the Declaration of Independence on July 4, 1776. His large signature is famous today.

Thomas Jefferson

April 13, 1743—July 4, 1826

Thomas Jefferson was a lawmaker from Virginia. He was a wealthy landowner and well educated, with expert knowledge in horticulture, philosophy, and science. Jefferson served as a delegate to the Second Continental Congress, and was the main author of the Declaration of Independence, which he signed on July 4, 1776.

After the American Revolution, Jefferson served as a diplomat in France, and then as the first United States secretary of state under President George Washington from 1790 to 1793. He served as vice president under President John Adams from 1797 to 1801. Jefferson was then elected the third president of the United States. He served two terms, from 1801 to 1809.

After his many years of government service, Jefferson retired to his home at Monticello in Virginia. Because he believed the future of America rested in a well-educated populace, he founded the University of Virginia in Charlottesville in 1819. Jefferson died on the same day as his friend and fellow Patriot John Adams, on July 4, 1826.

Benjamin Franklin

January 17, 1706—April 17, 179

Benjamin Franklin was a diplomat, inventor, and publisher. He was born and raised in Boston, Massachusetts, but spent most of his adult life in Philadelphia, Pennsylvania. He was successful in almost everything he set his mind to. As a scientist, he was especially interested in electricity. Many of his inventions, such as lightning rods and bifocal eyeglasses, benefit us to this day.

Franklin represented Pennsylvania in the Second Continental Congress, and helped write the Declaration of Independence. In 1778 he negotiated a military alliance with France, which was critical to the United States winning the war against Great Britain. As the U.S. ambassador to France, Franklin also helped negotiate the Treaty of Paris, which officially ended the Revolutionary War in 1783.

Patrick Henry

May 29, 1736—June 6, 1799

Patrick Henry was a Virginia lawyer and politician famous for his firebrand speeches promoting American independence. Elected to the First and Second Continental Congresses, Henry spoke often about uniting the colonies and opposing British rule. "The distinctions," he said, "between Virginians, Pennsylvanians, New Yorkers and New Englanders are no more. I am not a Virginian, but an American."

Henry had a talent for expressing his feelings about government and liberty in speeches that swayed many people to support the Patriot cause. On March 23, 1775, Henry spoke to fellow lawmakers in the Virginia House of Burgesses, who were trying to decide whether to prepare for war against Great Britain. "I know not what course others may take," Henry said, "but as for me, give me liberty or give me death!"

Thomas Paine was a writer of essays and pamphlets. His Patriot views strongly influenced Americans to support independence from Great Britain. His most influential work was a 50-page pamphlet called *Common Sense*, in which he argued that common people had the right to govern themselves, and that the tyranny of British rule could only be broken by full independence. *Common Sense* was a huge bestseller in all 13 colonies.

During the darkest days of the war in late 1776, when defeat seemed certain, Paine published a pamphlet called *The American Crisis* to lift the spirits of his fellow Patriots. "These are the times that try men's souls," Paine wrote. "The summer soldier and the sunshine patriot will, in this crisis, shrink from the service of their country; but he that stands it now, deserves the love and thanks of man and woman."

PATRIOT MILITARY LEADERS

Horatio Gates

July 26, 1727—
April 10, 1806

Horatio Gates was a top American general during the war. He was born in England and trained in the British military. In the 1750s, he served in the French and Indian War. After retirement, he moved permanently to North America, settling on a plantation in Virginia.

When war broke out in 1775, Gates offered his services to General George Washington. Gates's wartime experience was invaluable in helping organize the country's new Continental Army.

In 1777, Gates was in overall command at the Battle of Saratoga in New York. It was a major American victory. In 1780, however, he was blamed for the crushing Patriot defeat in South Carolina at the Battle of Camden. Gates was replaced by General Nathanael Greene and returned home to Virginia.

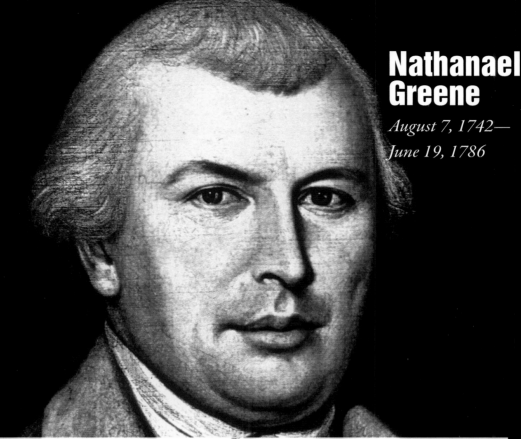

Nathanael Greene

August 7, 1742—
June 19, 1786

Nathanael Greene was one of the most important and successful generals of America's Continental Army. He was George Washington's most trusted and dependable officer. He started the war as a militia private from Rhode Island. After the siege of Boston, Massachusetts, he was promoted to the rank of brigadier general of the Continental Army in 1775. Greene and George Washington were the only two generals of the Continental Army who served throughout the entire war.

The troops under Greene's command fought in some of the most crucial struggles of the war. These included battles at Trenton, Princeton, Brandywine, Germantown, and Monmouth. His most famous fights came in the Southern colonies, including the Battle of Cowpens in South Carolina, and the Battle of Guilford Courthouse in North Carolina. Even when defeated, Greene inspired his troops, saying "We fight, get beaten, rise, and fight again."

Marquis de Lafayette

September 6, 1757—
May 20, 1834

The Marquis de Lafayette was a French noble who volunteered to serve in the Continental Army. He was an aide to General George Washington and an excellent officer. Lafayette was eventually promoted to general. Wounded in the leg at the Battle of Brandywine, Lafayette was nevertheless able to rally his troops in an orderly retreat, which saved many lives.

In 1779, Lafayette returned to France and urged the government to further support the American war effort. The following year he returned to America. He commanded three regiments of light infantry at the decisive victory over Great Britain at the Battle of Yorktown in Virginia.

Lafayette was one of many adventurous French volunteers who fought for the American cause. Toward the end of the war, more than 12,000 French troops and sailors joined the fight, under the overall command of Comte de Rochambeau. French help was critical to America winning freedom from British rule.

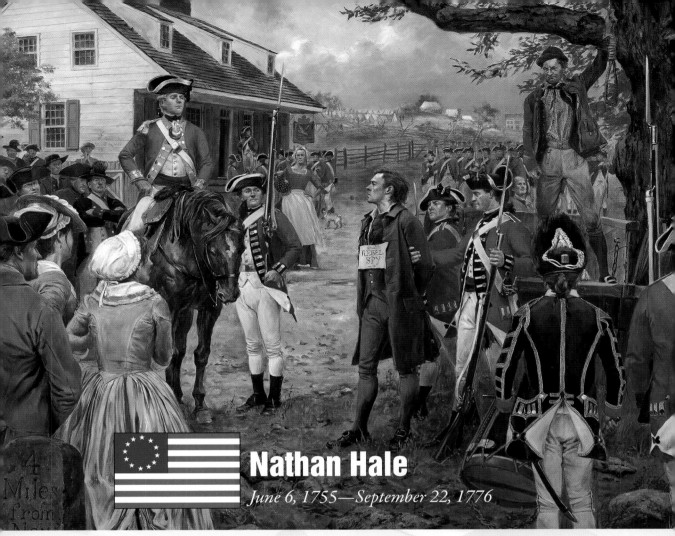

Nathan Hale

June 6, 1755—September 22, 1776

Nathan Hale was a young American military officer. Born in Coventry, Connecticut, he became a schoolteacher after graduating from Yale College in Connecticut. He joined the Patriot war effort early on, serving during the siege of Boston, Massachusetts. He was eventually promoted to captain in the Continental Army.

In 1776, Hale volunteered to spy on British forces occupying New York City. He dressed as a schoolmaster and began gathering information on British defenses and troop movements. He was captured by the British and sentenced to be hanged. Before his execution on September 22, 1776, Hale uttered the now-famous words, "I only regret that I have but one life to lose for my country!"

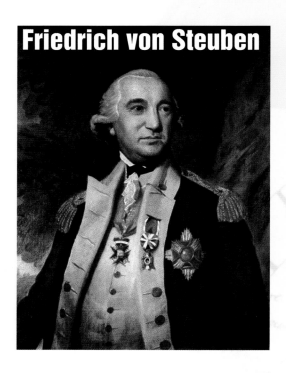

Friedrich von Steuben

Friedrich von Steuben (1730–1794) was a high-ranking officer from Prussia (part of today's Germany). He was a nobleman and a seasoned soldier. In 1777, he came to the United States. The following year, he volunteered his services to George Washington at Valley Forge, Pennsylvania. His experience in drilling troops and organizing the Continental Army were invaluable. He became an American citizen in 1784.

Benedict Arnold

In the early years of the American Revolution, Benedict Arnold (1741–1801) was a hero to the Patriot cause, winning battles at Fort Ticonderoga and Saratoga. He was a courageous fighter and leader of soldiers. However, Arnold grew jealous of his fellow officers. He also hated Congress. Amid financial troubles, Arnold changed sides and fought for the British. After the war, he left with his family for Great Britain.

Daniel Morgan (1736–1802) was a brigadier general of the Continental Army. He often led groups of rugged frontiersmen called "Morgan's Riflemen." They used accurate long rifles. Morgan was skilled at unconventional battlefield tactics, such as shooting at British officers to create confusion. His greatest victory was at the Battle of Cowpens, in which nearly 1,000 Redcoats were killed, wounded, or captured.

Daniel Morgan

Virginia frontiersman Brigadier General George Rogers Clark (1752–1818) fought in the wilderness area called the Old Northwest—today's Ohio, Illinois, and Indiana. Clark and his men captured forts at Vincennes and Kaskaskia. They also fought against Native Americans who were loyal to Great Britain. Clark's younger brother William gained fame in the Lewis and Clark Expedition.

George Rogers Clark

Anthony Wayne (1745–1796) was a brigadier general who fought British forces in several battles, including Monmouth and Yorktown. He had a fiery personality. He was brave, but sometimes he was so reckless that he earned the nickname "Mad Anthony." His greatest victory was a nighttime surprise attack at the Battle of Stony Point, New York.

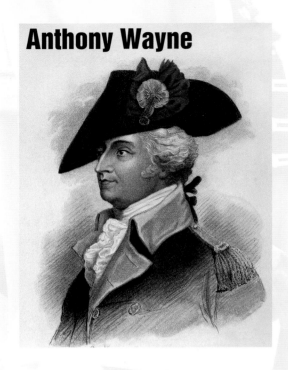

Anthony Wayne

Alexander Hamilton (1755–1804) is best known as the Founding Father who became the first Secretary of the Treasury. During the American Revolution, Hamilton served as an artilleryman for the New York militia. He later served as an aide to General George Washington. Given command of three infantry battalions, Hamilton fought bravely at the Battle of Yorktown, Virginia.

Alexander Hamilton

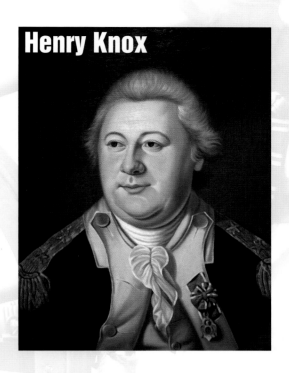

Henry Knox

Henry Knox (1750–1806) was a bookstore owner in Boston, Massachusetts, when war broke out. With his expert knowledge of cannons, he quickly rose through the ranks of the Continental Army to become a general in charge of artillery. Late in the winter of 1775–1776, Knox moved captured artillery from Fort Ticonderoga, New York, to Boston, Massachusetts, forcing British forces to flee the city.

Ethan Allen

Frontiersman Ethan Allen (1738–1789) settled in today's Vermont after fighting in the French and Indian War. Shortly after the American Revolution began in 1775, Allen gathered militia troops. Many were called the Green Mountain Boys, from Vermont. The group captured the British stronghold of Fort Ticonderoga in northeastern New York on May 10, 1775. He also fought during the invasion of Canada before being captured by the British.

BRITISH MILITARY LEADERS

Thomas Gage

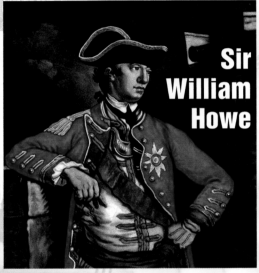

Sir William Howe

General Thomas Gage (1720–1787) was the commander of British forces in North America at the start of the American Revolution in 1775. He was also the military governor of Massachusetts. Gage's attempt to seize illegal weapons from colonial militias sparked the Battles of Lexington and Concord, marking the beginning of the war. After the disastrous Battle of Bunker Hill, Gage was replaced by Sir William Howe.

In October 1775, General Sir William Howe (1729–1814) took command of the British Army in North America. He was sympathetic to the Americans, but he was a military man who obeyed orders. Howe's forces won major victories in New York and Philadelphia, Pennsylvania, but some accused him of mismanaging the British war effort. Howe resigned in 1778 and returned to Great Britain.

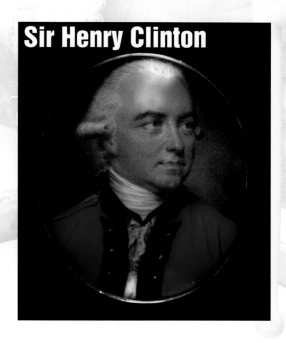

Sir Henry Clinton

General Sir Henry Clinton (1730–1795) took command of British forces on March 21, 1778, replacing Sir William Howe. Clinton was hobbled by a lack of British reinforcements, but managed to capture Charleston, South Carolina. After the major British defeat at Yorktown, Virginia, Clinton was replaced by Sir Guy Carleton in March 1782.

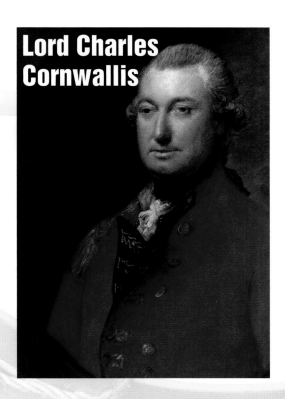

Lord Charles Cornwallis

General Lord Charles Cornwallis (1738–1805) was a skilled British battlefield commander. He won many victories, including the Battles of Brandywine and Charleston, but could never quite crush the American army. He was finally trapped by combined American and French forces at Yorktown, Virginia, and was forced to surrender. He returned to Great Britain after the war and continued to serve in government.

Molly Pitcher

WOMEN IN THE REVOLUTION

Although women did not hold official government office or serve in the military, they played many important roles in the American Revolution. In the years leading up to war, American women protested unfair British taxes by boycotting imported goods such as tea and fine clothing. In this way they proved that they, too, were Patriots. American women disrupted the British mercantile system by spinning cloth to sew their own clothes, or making basic goods such as soap.

During the war, the wives of many soldiers stayed on their farms and continued to work the land. This was important not only for the income, but also to feed the troops. Many women also spent their time manufacturing ammunition for the Continental Army.

Other women followed the armies as they marched across the countryside from battle to battle. Called "camp followers," these women sold goods to the troops, washed clothes, or performed other services.

Some women actually fought in battle, although this was extremely unusual. More commonly, women spied on British troops and passed along secrets to the Patriots. This was a very dangerous undertaking, since spies were usually executed by hanging.

Betsy Ross

Some women of the American Revolution became famous for their efforts. In 1777, when George Washington needed a national flag for the new United States, he sought help from Philadelphia, Pennsylvania, seamstress Betsy Ross (1752–1836). The result was the familiar "star-spangled banner" of red and white stripes and a blue field of 13 stars (representing the 13 original colonies) arranged in a circle. The story may or may not be true, but it has passed into American legend.

Another familiar story is that of Molly Pitcher, the nickname of Mary Ludwig Hays McCauly (1744–1832). At the 1778 Battle of Monmouth, in New Jersey, McCauly brought water to battle-fatigued soldiers. She also manned the cannon of her fallen husband during the fighting. After the Patriot victory, George Washington made McCauly a non-commissioned officer in the Continental Army.

The story of Molly Pitcher may actually be folklore, or the collected experiences of several real women who performed similar battlefield duties. Whatever the truth may be, her story represents the fighting spirit of American Patriot women throughout the young United States.

GLOSSARY

ARTILLERY
Large weapons of war, such as cannons, used by military forces.

BOSTON TEA PARTY
A protest against British tax policies staged by the Sons of Liberty in Boston, Massachusetts. On December 16, 1773, a group of colonists, some disguised as Native Americans, boarded three British ships docked in Boston Harbor. They used hatchets to open 342 chests of tea, then dumped the contents into the water.

BOYCOTT
A refusal to buy something in order to show disapproval.

COLONY
A group of people who settle in a distant territory but remain citizens of their native country.

COMMITTEES OF CORRESPONDENCE
Unofficial "shadow governments" organized by the 13 colonies to plan resistance to British rule.

FRENCH AND INDIAN WAR
A war fought between 1754-1763 in North America between the forces of France and Great Britain and the two countries's Native American allies. It was part of a larger worldwide conflict called the Seven Years' War.

HARVARD
America's first university, located in Cambridge, Massachusetts. It opened in 1636.

House of Burgesses

An assembly of elected representatives in Virginia that passed laws and regulations.

Mercantile System

A system of trading between colonies and the mother country. The American colonies were a source of tremendous profit for Great Britain. Raw materials, such as rice and molasses, were shipped to Great Britain. In return, manufactured British goods were bought by the colonists.

Militia

Citizens who were part-time soldiers rather than professional army fighters. Militiamen, such as the Minutemen from Massachusetts, usually fought only in their local areas and continued with their normal jobs when they were not needed.

Parliament

The law-making body of Great Britain. It consists of the House of Lords and the House of Commons.

Patriots

Colonists who rebelled against Great Britain during the American Revolution.

Redcoats

The name that was often given to British soldiers because part of their uniform included a bright red coat.

Sons of Liberty

A group of Patriot colonists who banded together to oppose the Stamp Act, Townshend Acts, and other oppressive laws imposed by Great Britain.

INDEX